MIGHTY ANIMAL MIGRATIONS

A SEAL'S JOURNEY

David and Julie Lavender

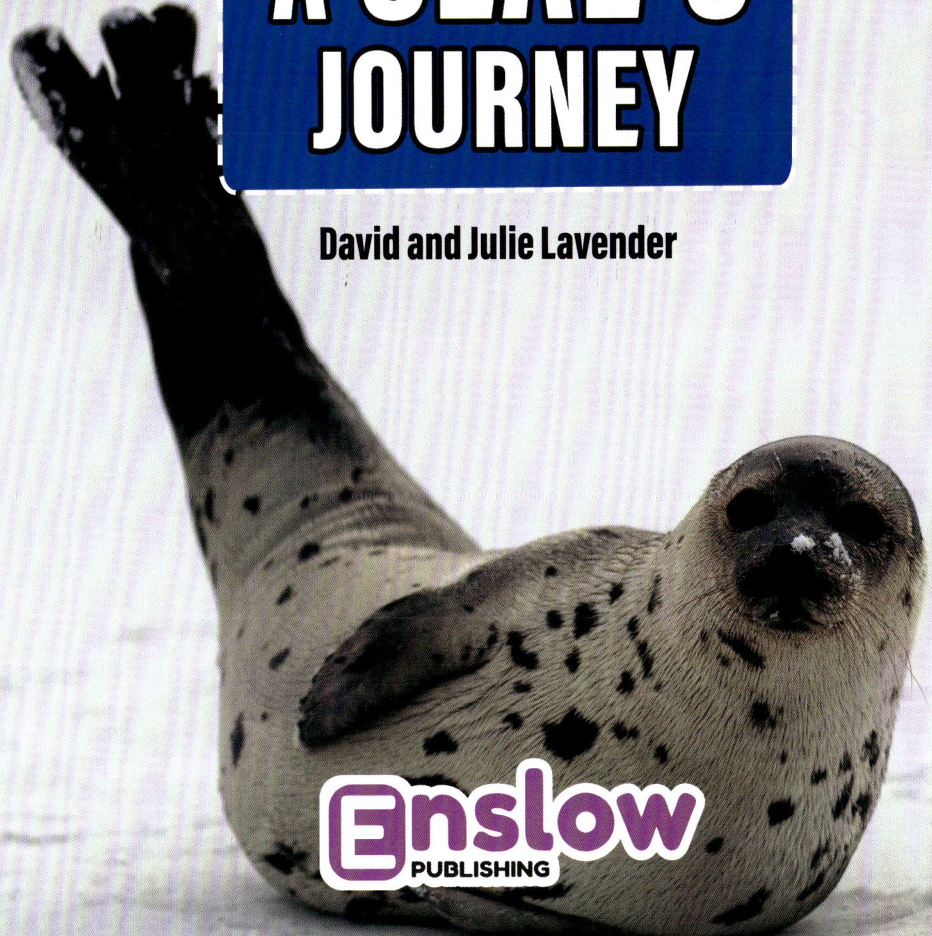

Enslow PUBLISHING

Please visit our website, www.enslow.com. For a free color catalog of all our high-quality books, call toll free 1-800-398-2504 or fax 1-877-980-4454

Published in 2027 by
Enslow Publishing
2544 Clinton Street
Buffalo, NY 14224

Cataloging-in-Publication Data
Names: Lavender, David R., 1961-, author. | Lavender, Julie, author.
Title: A seal's journey / by David and Julie Lavender.
Description: Buffalo, NY : Enslow Publishing, 2027. | Series: Mighty animal migrations | Includes glossary.
Identifiers: ISBN 9781978549630 (pbk.) | ISBN 9781978549647 (library bound) | ISBN 9781978549654 (ebook)
Subjects: LCSH: Harp seal--Juvenile literature. | Seals (Animals)--Behavior--Juvenile literature.
Classification: LCC QL737.P64 L384 2027 | DDC 599.7929--dc23

Photo credits: Cover, p 1, Dolores M. Harvey/Shutterstock.com; background used throughout interior, detchana wangkheeree/AdobeStock.com; Calendars used throught interior, Evolvect/AdobeStock.com; p 4, Agami Photo Agency/Shutterstock.com; p 5, Neil Benison Photography/Shutterstock.com; p 6, Vladimir Melnik/Shutterstock.com; p 7, 24, Dolores M. Harvey/Shutterstock.com; p 8, 9, Vladimir Melnik/Shutterstock.com; p 10, 11, WilliamRoggero/Shutterstock.com; p 12, 13, 14, 15, Dolores M. Harvey/Shutterstock.com; p 16, @Wiki; p 17, ohrim/Shutterstock.com, Thomas Roell/Shutterstock.com; p 18, miroslav chytil/Shutterstock.com; p 19, Daniel Toh/Shutterstock.com; p 20, 21, Dolores M. Harvey/Shutterstock.com; p 22, Vladimir Melnik/Shutterstock.com; p 23, @Wiki; p 25, The physio/Shutterstock.com; p 27, karenfoleyphotography/Shutterstock.com; p 29, Peter Hermes Furian/Shutterstock.com

Printed in China

CPSIA compliance information: Batch #QSENS27: For further information, contact Enslow Publishing, New York, New York, at 1-800-398-2504.

Table of Contents

An Arctic Journey

Millions of animals migrate long distances each year. They search for food, better living conditions, or a safe place to birth their young.

Many migrations take place over land. Some animals swim through the sea on their migration. Other animals migrate over land and water.

Some animals, like the harp seal, make long, dangerous journeys in the freezing waters of the Arctic Ocean. The harp seal depends on the ice to breed and find food. It follows the ice as it melts in the summer. Harp seals migrate thousands of miles every year.

Really Cool News

Three different populations of harp seals migrate each year. The largest population, the Northwest Atlantic group, lives in the waters between Eastern Canada and western Greenland. The Greenland Sea population lives on the east side of Greenland. The Barents Sea population lives off the north coast of Russia.

Harp Seal Pup

On a cold morning in February, a mother harp seal gives birth to a newborn pup. The harp seal pup is born on **pack ice** off the coast of northeast Newfoundland.

At first, her fur looks yellow. That's from being inside the mother harp seal. But in three days, the pup's fur turns pure white.

The harp seal depends on her thick fur to stay warm. Temperatures stay below freezing most of the time. Blowing winds make it even colder. The pup's white fur soaks up the sun's rays and keeps her warm.

Really Cool News

Harp seals get their name from the black mark on the back of adult seals. The black fur is shaped like a harp musical instrument. Some scientists think it looks like a saddle. Harp seals are also called saddleback seals. The harp is more noticeable on an adult male seal.

Gaining Weight

The newborn pup drinks milk from her mother. The mother's milk is rich in fat. The harp seal pup gains about five pounds (2.2 kg) a day. She adds a layer of **blubber** under her skin.

The harp seal's long white fur traps a layer of air that **insulates** the newborn pup. The blubber layer insulates the pup too. It also stores energy.

When the mother seal isn't nursing her pup, she leaves the pack ice to swim in the cold water. She stays close by and comes back often to nurse the newborn seal.

Many Moms, Many Pups

The young harp seal is not the only newborn on the pack ice. Thousands of female harp seals **haul out** onto the same chunk of ice to deliver their babies. Many other white-furred harp seal pups surround her.

The young harp seal is hungry and barks for her mother to come feed her. She barks again and again. She's ready to eat.

The mother seal leaves the water and finds her pup in the crowd of seals. She knows the sound of her offspring's bark. And she recognizes her smell too.

Really Cool News

The bond between a mother harp seal and her offspring is strong. She learns her pup's scent and bark quickly. By the time they are adults, harp seals can make 17 different sounds to communicate with other harp seals.

Left on the Ice

When the newborn pup is 12 days old, the mother harp seal leaves. She stops nursing her pup and swims away. The **weaned** pup is on her own. She stays very still on the ice to conserve energy.

In two weeks, the harp seal pup begins to **molt**. She loses her white fur. New, silvery gray fur grows in.

The harp seal pup stays on the ice for six weeks. With nothing to eat, she loses half her weight.

Really Cool News

Most newborn harp seals weigh about 25 pounds (11 kg) at birth. When the mother harp seal stops nursing her pup, the new harp seal weighs about 80 pounds (36 kg). Harp seal pups need that extra weight to survive alone when mother seals leave them.

A Hungry Pup

Hunger forces the harp seal pup to the water. She glides into the cold water headfirst. She pulls back on her flippers and moves her tail. The harp seal pup is learning to swim.

At first, she stays close to the edge of the ice. She dives a little deeper to find food. She nibbles on her very first shrimp. The harp seal pup tries to catch a crab but misses.

She tries again and again. Finally, she succeeds. The harp seal pup eats shrimp, crabs, and small lobsters until she is full.

Really Cool News

Harp seals have large eyes that help them see well under water. Whiskers on each side of their snout sense movement, leading them to **prey** or helping them avoid danger.

Following the Ice

When summer comes, pack ice chunks melt in the south where it's warmer. It's time for the harp seal's first migration. She'll need to follow the pack ice as it moves north into the Arctic Ocean.

The harp seal pup moves into the Labrador Sea with other harp seals. She's mastered swimming and diving. She catches squid and krill. She munches on redfish, halibut, and cod. She gobbles up herring.

Suddenly, a Greenland shark dashes toward the harp seal pup. The shark swims fast, but the pup turns quickly. She dives deep. She just barely avoids the shark's sharp teeth.

Greenland shark

Really Cool News

Harp seals face other dangers besides predators. Sometimes they get hit by ships. Harp seals get tangled in fishing nets or large pieces of trash in the water. At times, they may swim into an oil spill. And some are hunted for their fur or as food.

Watching Out for Danger

The harp seal pup keeps moving north. She dives and searches for food in the Davis Strait. Fish are plentiful here. She eats Arctic cod and catches large crabs.

In a flash, a killer whale speeds toward the harp seal. The whale flashes a mouth full of large teeth. The whale swims fast, but the harp seal darts and turns quickly. She leaps onto the pack ice to escape the killer whale. She's safe for now.

Soon, the harp seal moves into Baffin Bay. She rests on the pack ice. Movement alerts the harp seal. A polar bear scares her back into the water.

polar bear

killer whale (orca)

Really Cool News

Killer whales, also known as orcas, are a major predator in ocean waters. They can weigh up to 11 tons (10 mt) and swim as fast as 30 miles (48 km) per hour. Killer whales have the second-largest brain of all ocean mammals.

Heading South

Now that summer is over, cooler weather returns. More and more ice returns as the water gets colder and colder. It's time for the harp seal to migrate south.

Adult and young harp seals leave Baffin Bay and journey through Davis Strait. They head toward Labrador Sea. The seals swim back to the pupping place where they were born.

Harp seals travel and hunt for food with other harp seals. They move around and live in large groups. They're rarely alone. Harp seals are **social** animals.

Really Cool News

Harp seals often swim on their backs. Scientists aren't really sure why they do this. Because their eyes are near the top of their head, scientists wonder if they swim on their backs to watch for prey in the water below them.

Back Where She Started

The young harp seal makes it back to the same spot where she was born. She hauls out on the pack ice with other young seals.

Thousands of pregnant harp seals haul out on the pack ice too. In just a couple of days, they'll deliver newborn harp seals.

The young harp seal won't be ready to mate and have her own pups until she's about four years old.

Really Cool News

Male harp seals, called bulls, fight other male harp seals for the chance to mate with a female. They use their front flippers to fight. They also use large teeth to bite. Once harp seals mate, the female will deliver a newborn pup in about 11 months.

Another Molt

The one-year-old harp seal swims to another chunk of pack ice. She hauls out on the ice to molt. Her fur falls out in patches.

By now, she has a thick layer of blubber under her skin to keep her warm. In a couple of weeks, new fur grows in. She'll need the healthy coat of fur and a thick blubber layer for the journey north.

It's time to migrate again.

Cold Arctic Journeys

Harp seals live in the cold waters of the North Atlantic Ocean and Arctic Ocean. Life begins for harp seals on a large chunk of pack ice at the southernmost point of their migration route.

When summer weather melts pack ice in the south, the harp seals migrate north to follow the ice and find food. They eat fish, shrimp, and other prey. They look out for predators like sharks, killer whales, and polar bears.

When winter brings more pack ice, harp seals migrate south again. Their dangerous migration covers more than 3,000 miles (4,828 km) in freezing cold ocean waters.

A Seal Migration Map

1. A harp seal pup is born on pack ice off the coast of northeast Newfoundland.
2. The harp seal pup leaves the pack ice to search for food. She swims north by way of the Labrador Sea.
3. The harp seal makes her way through the Davis Strait, catching and eating prey along the way.
4. The harp seal moves into Baffin Bay and continues to feed.
5. When colder temperatures cause new ice to form, the harp seal migrates south. She leaves Baffin Bay and swims through Davis Strait.
6. The harp seal swims through Labrador Sea and makes it back to her birthplace off the coast of northeast Newfoundland.

GREENLAND
ICELAND
Denmark Strait
Baffin Bay
Arctic Circle
Baffin Island
Davis Strait
LABRADOR SEA
LABRADOR
CANADA
NEWFOUNDLAND
Gulf of St. Lawrence

Glossary

blubber (BLUHB-ur): a layer of fat under the skin that helps animals stay warm

haul out (hawl out): when an animal like a seal or walrus climbs out of the sea water onto ice or land

insulates (IN-suh-lates): to protect an animal from cold or heat with a covering or substance, like blubber

molt (mohlt): when an animal sheds its outer covering of fur, feathers, or skin

pack ice (pak ise): a large mass of floating sea ice made up of many small pieces of ice frozen together

prey (pray): an animal that is hunted and eaten by other animals

social (SOH-shuhl): animals that live together with animals of the same kind in organized groups

weaned (weend): when a young animal is no longer dependent on its mother's milk

Fact Check

1. Harp seals depend on fur and _______ to stay warm.
   a. blubber   b. whiskers   c. flippers

2. A harp seal mother recognizes her pup by sound and ______.
   a. color of eyes   b. shape of tail   c. smell

3. Harp seals get their name from a __________.
   a. mark on their back   b. sound their flippers make   c. food they eat

Answers: 1. a, 2. c, 3. a

Further Reading

Bahn, Christopher. *Amazing Animals: Seals*. The Creative Company, 2025.

Grady, Tyler. *Arctic Animals*. Dylanna Publishing, Inc., 2024.

Lavender, Julie and David. *Spotlight on Nature: Seal*. The Creative Company, 2025.

On the Internet

Arctic Seals

https://kids.nationalgeographic.com/animals/mammals/facts/harp-seal

See adorable seal photos, learn facts and information, and see a map of the harp seal's range at the top of the globe.

Harp Seal Facts for Kids

https://kids.nationalgeographic.com/animals/mammals/facts/harp-seal

Learn the scientific name for the harp seal and learn more about the harp seal's migration, travel, and life cycle.

Publisher's note to educators and parents: Our editors have carefully reviewed these websites to ensure that they are suitable for students. Many websites change frequently, however, and we cannot guarantee that a site's future contents will continue to meet our high standards of quality and educational value. Be advised that students should be closely supervised whenever they access the internet.

Index

About the Authors

David and Julie Lavender had a migration of their own while David served as a medical entomologist for the United States Navy. During their 20 years as a military family, they moved from Georgia to Florida to North Carolina to Florida to Virginia to California to Washington and back to Georgia. The Lavenders lived in nine homes in six states. They loved meeting friends and searching for wildlife with each new address. David's careers included working with animals as an entomologist and wildlife biologist, and Julie loved educating kids as a teacher and homeschooling mom.